PEOPLE

I NFO PICS

BY HARRIET BRUNDLE

BookLife
PUBLISHING

©2019
BookLife Publishing Ltd.
King's Lynn
Norfolk PE30 4LS

All rights reserved.
Printed in Malaysia.

A catalogue record for this
book is available from the
British Library.

ISBN: 978-1-78637-916-0

Written by:
Harriet Brundle

Edited by:
Emilie Dufresne

Designed by:
Danielle Rippengill

Image Credits

Cover and throughout – maximmmmum, Sira Anamwong. 4&5 – Colorcocktail, PremiumArt, Julia Tim.
6&7 – GoodVector. 8&9 – ONYXprj, Antun Hirsman, MicroOne. 10&11 – asantosg. 12&13 – ONYXprj,
Antun Hirsman, MicroOne. 14&15 – art4all, Beresnev. 16&17 – Sapann Design. 18&19 – MSSA. 20&21 –
bioraven, Sudowoodo. 22&23 – Tetiana Yurchenko. All images courtesy of Shutterstock.com.
With thanks to Getty Images, Thinkstock Photo and iStockphoto.

CONTENTS

Words that look like <u>this</u> can be found in the glossary on page 24.

PEOPLE

The number of people that live on Earth is always changing.

At the moment, over 7 billion people live on planet Earth.

4

The number of people on Earth has been rising for years. It is thought it will keep on rising in the future.

Every person speaks a language and is part of a <u>community</u>.

POPULATION

The population is the number of people living in one place.

The population will be different in villages, towns, cities and countries around the world.

Some places on Earth have a high population, which means they have lots of people living there.

Other places have a low population, which means only a small number of people live there.

Indonesia, Brazil and the US are countries which have a high population.

India has the second-highest population of any country. It is thought that there are over 1 billion people living there.

US

Pacific Ocean

Atlantic Ocean

Brazil

Southern Ocean

Arctic
Ocean

Vatican City

China

Pacific
Ocean

Indonesia

Tuvalu

India

Indian
Ocean

Nauru

China has the highest population on Earth. Nearly one and a half billion people live in China.

Vatican City, Tuvalu and Nauru are some countries with very low populations.

9

RELIGIONS

Different people follow different religions all around the world.

There are lots of different religions and each has their own beliefs and practices.

It's thought that around three-tenths of the world's population follow Christianity.

Over two-tenths of the world's population follow Islam.

Other popular religions include Buddhism, Judaism, Hinduism and Sikhism.

Some people don't believe in any god. This is known as being an atheist.

TRANSPORT

Every day, people travel to and from different places. To do so, they may need to use transport.

Cars, buses and aeroplanes are examples of types of transport.

It's thought that on one particularly busy day, there were over 200,000 flights across the world.

The London Underground is an underground railway. Up to 5 million people make journeys using the London Underground every day.

There are over 1 billion cars in the world.

Some people might choose to travel by boat, bicycle or tram.

PASSPORT

HOMES

People live in different homes around the world.

In busy towns and cities, people may live in houses which are closer together.

High-rise buildings often have lots of flats or apartments so that many people can live there.

It is thought that around 26 million people live in the city of Shanghai in China.

People might live in cottages, houseboats or houses on <u>stilts</u>.

Fewer people live in villages so houses might be farther apart.

People can make their homes in many different places, such as on mountains and beaches or next to rivers.

LANGUAGES

Around the world there are thousands of different languages spoken.

It is thought that the most-spoken language in the world is Mandarin Chinese.

Some people speak more than one language.

Hello!

Salve!

Zdravstvuyte!

BODIES

People might speak different languages, live in different countries and all look different. But inside we are very similar.

An adult **skeleton** has more than 200 bones.

We have more bones when we are born but some **fuse** together as we get older.

18

Your brain is the control centre for your body.

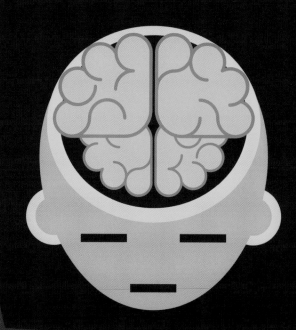

It is <u>responsible</u> for your thought, speech, movement, memory and many more jobs.

Your heart is roughly the size of your fist.

Your heart usually beats around once every second for your whole life.

RECORD-BREAKING PEOPLE

Some human bodies have been able to set amazing records.

The longest tongue ever measured was over ten centimetres.

It's thought the tallest man to have ever lived was over two and a half metres tall.

One man managed to grow the fingernails on one of his hands to 985 centimetres.

GETTING TOGETHER

Every year, people all over the world get together to take part in different events.

PROTEST PROTEST

Religious gatherings make up many of these events. These might include marriages, funerals, pilgrimages or festivals.

Millions of people have taken part in protests or marches all over the world.

NO!

The largest gathering of people dressed as Superman happened in the UK, and 867 people took part.

In Australia, a group of 1,869 people hold the record for being the largest group of people to stargaze at the same time.

GLOSSARY

community	a group of people who are connected by something
festivals	days or periods of celebration
fuse	join together
pilgrimages	long trips or journeys usually to do with religion
practices	ways of doing things
protests	events where large groups of people show their dislike of a certain thing together
responsible	in charge of doing certain things
skeleton	the framework of bones supporting the body
stilts	poles that are used to hold something up

INDEX

24